HABITAT
SURVIVAL

FORESTS

Claire Llewellyn

Raintree

www.raintreepublishers.co.uk
Visit our website to find out
more information about
Raintree books.

To order:
☎ Phone 0845 6044371
🖹 Fax +44 (0) 1865 312263
💻 Email myorders@raintreepublishers.co.uk

Customers from outside the UK please telephone +44 1865 312262

Raintree is an imprint of Capstone Global Library
Limited, a company incorporated in England and
Wales having its registered office at 7 Pilgrim Street,
London, EC4V 6LB – Registered company number:
6695582

Edited by Nancy Dickmann, Kristen Kowalkowski,
  and Claire Throp
Designed by Philippa Jenkins
Original illustrations © Capstone Global Library Ltd
  2013
Illustrations by Oxford Designers and Illustrators,
  and Jeff Edwards
Picture research by Tracy Cummins
Originated by Capstone Global Library Ltd
Printed and bound in China by CTPS

ISBN 978 1 406 23991 1 (hardback)
16 15 14 13 12
10 9 8 7 6 5 4 3 2 1

ISBN 978 1 406 24001 6 (paperback)
17 16 15 14 13
10 9 8 7 6 5 4 3 2 1

British Library Cataloguing in Publication Data
Llewellyn, Claire.
Forests. -- (Habitat survival)
577.3-dc23
A full catalogue record for this book is available from
the British Library.

Acknowledgements
We would like to thank the following for permission
to reproduce photographs: Agefotostock p. 16
(© ARCO/D. Usher); FLPA pp. 8 (ImageBroker/
Imagebroker), 12 (Donald M. Jones/Minden
Pictures), 13 (Mark Sisson), 20 (Chien Lee/Minden
Pictures), 21 (Suzi Eszterhas/Minden Pictures), 22
(Cyril Ruoso/Minden Pictures), 24 (Konrad Wothe/
Minden Pictures), 27 (Paul Sawer), 29 (Murray
Cooper/Minden Pictures); iStockphoto p. 15
(© Aleksander Bolbot); Nature Picture Library
p. 28 (Eric Baccega); Shutterstock pp. 4 (© Rob
Christiaans), 5 (© Poznyakov), 7 (© Andrew Roland),
10 (© Fokin Oleg), 11 (© sunnyfrog), 17 (© Irishman),
19 (© Dr. Morley Read), 25 (© Mary Terriberry), 26
(© Lisette van der Hoorn).

Cover photograph of a toucan reproduced with
permission of Shutterstock/Vitaly Romanovich.

Every effort has been made to contact copyright
holders of any material reproduced in this book. Any
omissions will be rectified in subsequent printings if
notice is given to the publisher.

Disclaimer
All the internet addresses (URLs) given in this book
were valid at the time of going to press. However,
due to the dynamic nature of the internet, some
addresses may have changed, or sites may have
changed or ceased to exist since publication. While
the author and publisher regret any inconvenience
this may cause readers, no responsibility for any such
changes can be accepted by either the author or the
publisher.

Contents

Some words are shown in bold, **like this**. You can find out what they mean by looking in the glossary.

What are forests?

Forests are big areas of land where trees grow close together, along with other kinds of plants. There are different kinds of forest around the world. This is because different **climates** suit different types of trees.

Forest life

Forests are important **habitats**. They provide animals with shelter and food. In fact, the more food a forest provides, the more kinds of animals will live in it. Many different animals live in the world's forests, from reindeer and wolves in the far north to tigers and snakes in the **tropics**.

Red deer live on the edges of **coniferous** forests. They feed on grasses, bushes, and young trees.

This book looks at how plants and animals have **adapted** to life in the forest and how they depend on one another to survive. It examines how humans affect forests and how our actions can threaten forest life or help it to survive.

All sorts of life

Most forests contain a huge variety of plant and animal life. For example, scientists found 10,500 different kinds of animals and plants in a single forest in Switzerland.

Forests around the world

In the far north, where it is bitterly cold, forests are made up of **evergreen** trees, such as firs and pines. Further south, where it is milder and wetter, forests contain more types of plants, and the trees lose their leaves in winter. In the **tropics**, there are steamy forests with tall trees and plants of every kind.

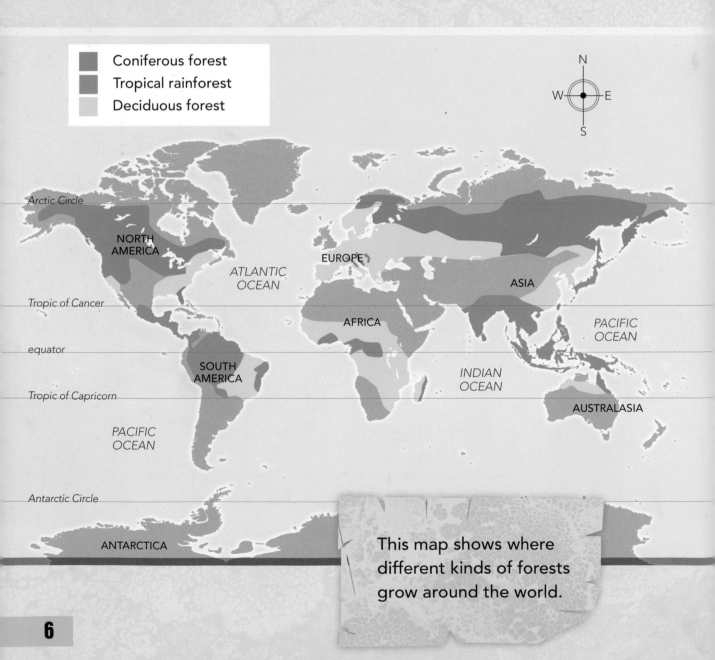

Coniferous forest
Tropical rainforest
Deciduous forest

N
W E
S

Arctic Circle

NORTH AMERICA

EUROPE

ASIA

ATLANTIC OCEAN

PACIFIC OCEAN

Tropic of Cancer

AFRICA

equator

SOUTH AMERICA

INDIAN OCEAN

Tropic of Capricorn

AUSTRALASIA

PACIFIC OCEAN

Antarctic Circle

ANTARCTICA

This map shows where different kinds of forests grow around the world.

A temperate forest changes in autumn. The leaves on the trees slowly change colour and begin to fall to the ground.

Forest layers

Forests have different layers, rather like the floors in a building. On the ground, there are flowers and ferns. Next, there is the **understorey**. It contains shrubs, small trees, **lichen**, and moss. At the top, the branches of the tallest trees make a green **canopy** over the forest. The different layers are home to different animals – from squirrels and monkeys high in the branches to beetles and worms on the ground.

Temperate rainforests

A different kind of rainforest grows in some cool, wet places, such as the north Pacific coast of the United States. These forests contain lush ferns and towering evergreen trees, which are covered with lichen and moss. They are called **temperate** rainforest.

The forest jigsaw

Everything in a forest depends on everything else. It is rather like a jigsaw made with four important pieces:

1. Plants: Plants use sunlight, air, and water to make food. They make leaves, bark, flowers, fruits, and seeds.

2. Plant-eaters: Caterpillars, squirrels, deer, and many other animals eat the forest plants. They eat leaves, bark, flowers, berries, and nuts, as well as **lichen** and moss.

3. Meat-eaters: Spiders, owls, and many other animals eat the plant-eaters. They hunt smaller meat-eating animals, too.

4. Decomposers: When they die, animals and plants rot away with the help of **decomposers**, such as fungi, earthworms, and slugs. They turn dead things into **nutrients** for plants.

Owls are meat-eaters. They feed on small **mammals**, such as mice and voles.

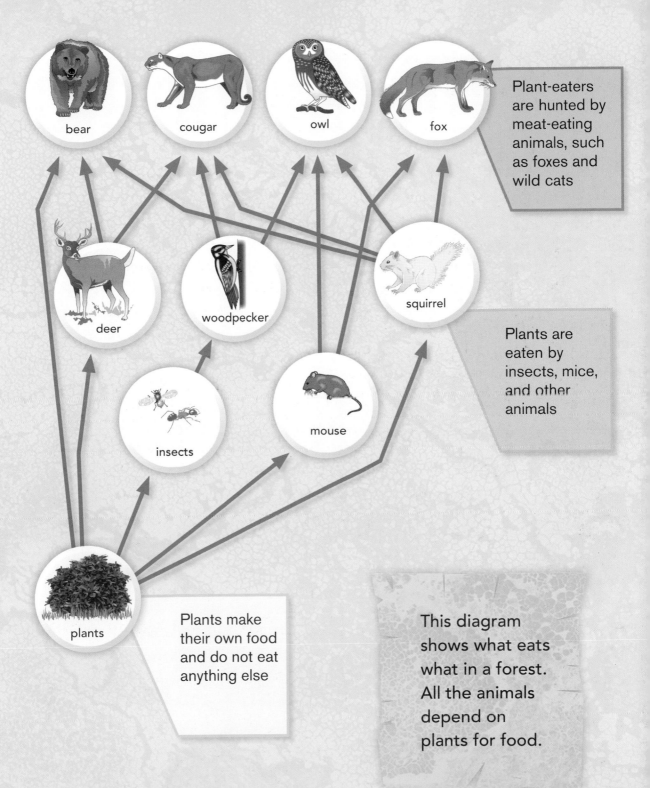

bear

cougar

owl

fox

Plant-eaters are hunted by meat-eating animals, such as foxes and wild cats

deer

woodpecker

squirrel

insects

mouse

Plants are eaten by insects, mice, and other animals

plants

Plants make their own food and do not eat anything else

This diagram shows what eats what in a forest. All the animals depend on plants for food.

Coniferous forests

In the far north, a huge **evergreen** forest grows. The trees are all **conifers**, such as fir and pine, and the forests are called **coniferous** forests. These trees do not grow flowers. Instead, they produce woody cones, which contain seeds.

Adapting to the cold

The conifers in northern forests have **adapted** to survive the bitter cold. They have sloping branches to shed the snow and needle-shaped leaves with a tough, waxy skin. These help the trees to lock in water, which is scarce in winter.

Northern forests contain only a few kinds of tree but they grow in vast numbers.

Conifers are different from other kinds of trees. They have needle-like leaves and woody cones.

On the ground

In northern forests, the ground is frozen for many months of the year. The surface of the soil **thaws** in summer, making the ground wet and spongy. It is covered with a thick mat of old pine needles. **Lichens** grow on the ground and on the branches of the trees.

Southern forests?

Conifers do grow south of the **equator** but there are no huge coniferous forests. This is because the land here is too warm.

Animals in coniferous forests

Coniferous forests are not easy places for animals to live. There is very little food to eat and the winters are long and cold.

Pine needles are not good to eat so plant-eaters, such as squirrels and birds, feed on the seeds inside the cones. Reindeer feed on **lichen** and moss. A reindeer's hooves are shaped like shovels to dig for lichen under the snow.

Crossbills have a crossed beak that works like a lever to open cones.

Meat-eaters

Coniferous forests are home to pine martens. These fast animals chase birds and squirrels through the trees. They grip the bark with their strong claws, and their long tail helps them to balance as they leap from branch to branch. On the ground there are other hunters, such as wolves and bears.

Pine martens have **good sight** and hearing, and are well **adapted** to life in the trees.

Hiding food

Some birds hide seeds to last them through the winter. A nutcracker hides about 30,000 seeds a year in up to 5,000 different places! It remembers where most of them are and the ones it forgets may grow into trees.

Deciduous forests

South of the **coniferous** forests, there is a milder **climate** with plenty of rain. Forests have a greater mix of trees, such as oak, maple, ash, and beech. These trees grow broad, flat leaves, which fall to the ground in winter. They are called **deciduous** trees.

Leaves and roots

Deciduous trees grow new leaves in the spring. The trees have a spreading shape, which allows their leaves to reach the light. This provides them with **energy** to grow. Far below, in the ground, long roots suck up water and **nutrients** from the soil.

Energy from the Sun

A plant's leaves use sunlight, air, and water to make food.

Leaves take in **carbon dioxide** from the air

Roots take up water and nutrients

The damp forest floor is home to mosses and fungi.

The forest floor

In autumn, the days grow dark and there is not enough energy for the trees to grow. The leaves change colour and fall to the ground. As they rot, they provide nutrients for trees, ferns, and shrubs.

Rings in the trunk

A deciduous tree makes new wood every year during the spring and summer. This shows up inside the trunk as rings, which can be seen when the tree is cut down. In good growing years, the rings are thick. In poor years, they are thin.

Animals in deciduous forests

The trees in a **deciduous** forest provide animals with plenty of leaves, fruits, and seeds to eat. Many more animals live here than in a **coniferous** forest.

Insects and birds

Deciduous trees are full of insects, such as beetles and wasps. Their young, which are called larvae, are food for birds. Woodpeckers use their long bills to drill into the trunks of trees and spear larvae feeding inside.

By eating harmful pests, such as larvae, woodpeckers keep trees healthy.

Brown bears eat well in summer and autumn. They hibernate through the winter when there is not much food.

Forest mammals

Many **mammals** live in the forest, from squirrels and raccoons to weasels and deer. Bears spend most of their time on the ground but can climb trees to rest or feed. They eat almost every food the forest has to offer – nuts, honey, ants, eggs and chicks, and even young deer.

Is that a caterpillar?

Caterpillars are easy **prey** for birds so they try to defend themselves. Some look like buds or twigs. Others blend in so well with their surroundings that they are hard to see.

Tropical rainforests

Tropical rainforests grow near the **equator**, in places that are warm all year round. Most days provide sunshine and rain. This kind of **climate** is perfect for plants.

In the Sun

Most rainforest trees are **evergreens** with broad leaves and tall, straight trunks. Their branches make a sunlit **canopy**, which produces leaves, flowers, and fruits. Other plants, such as orchids, perch high on the trees to reach the light. Their roots do not grow in the soil, but take in water from the steamy air.

The different layers of the rainforest are home to different kinds of plants – from fungi on the forest floor to orchids high in the trees.

orchid

liana

Canopy

Understorey

Forest floor

In the shade

Below the canopy, in the **understorey**, there is shade and dappled light. Small palm trees and banana plants grow here. Lower still, on the damp forest floor, fungi recycle old leaves and logs into **nutrients** for plants.

Below the canopy, there are ferns and woody vines, called lianas, which wind up towards the light.

All sorts of trees

In an area of rainforest the size of a football pitch, you might find 180 different kinds of trees. In a **deciduous** forest, you might find 10. In a **coniferous** forest, you would be lucky to find three.

Rainforest animals

Rainforests are home to many different animals. They have **adapted** to life at the different levels of the forest.

Monkeys leap through the trees. Many can use their tail as an extra arm or leg, by wrapping it around the branches. Birds, bats, and butterflies fly from tree to tree. The flying lizard can glide, too. It stretches two flaps of skin, which work a bit like wings.

Hiding away

Animals need to stay hidden as they hunt for **prey**. Their skin or fur helps them to do this. Bold markings help the gaboon viper to hide in the leaves on the forest floor. Big cats have coats with spots or stripes. This helps them to blend in with the forest's dappled light.

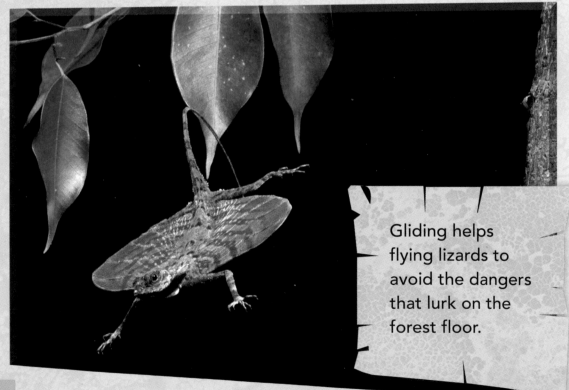

Gliding helps flying lizards to avoid the dangers that lurk on the forest floor.

The markings on a jaguar's coat blend in with the background, and make the cat harder to see.

On the ground

The forest floor is alive with creepy-crawlies. Armies of ants search for food. Large spiders, such as tarantulas, hunt for insects, frogs, and chicks. Deer and wild pigs search for leaves and roots.

Full of life

Tropical rainforests cover a very small area of Earth's surface. Yet scientists believe that they contain more than half of all the world's animals and plants.

Forest tribes

People have lived in rainforests for thousands of years, and they still do today. Some forest tribes move from place to place. Others live in villages. They depend on the forest for many things.

The Baka tribe lives in Cameroon, West Africa. They dry and weave the stalks and leaves of plants to make special costumes.

A world apart

About 200,000 people live in the rainforest in South America. Some live in such remote places that they have never had contact with the outside world.

Using plants

Forest people use hundreds of different plants. They use them to make their houses, clothes, and tools. They also collect them for medicines, fuel, and food. They gather pineapples, mangoes, nuts, and honey. They grow maize (corn) and other crops on small plots of land.

Catching animals

Forest people catch animals for food. They catch fish, gather insects, and hunt antelope, monkeys, and pigs. It takes great skill to stalk animals and shoot them with a bow and arrow, a spear, or **poisoned** dart. Forest people make their own poisons from poisonous animals or plants.

Damaging the forests

Humans are cutting down the world's forests. We use the wood to burn as fuel, to make buildings and furniture, and to make paper and card. We also clear forests to use the land for new houses and roads. All kinds of forests are disappearing but tropical rainforests are in the greatest danger. Huge areas are cleared every year to make way for factories, mines, and farms. You now find cattle grazing on land where there was once thick forest.

When people cut down and burn tropical forests, animal and plant **habitats** are destroyed.

Acid rain threatens all kinds of forests. This problem is growing worse as there is more industry and more air pollution around the world.

Acid rain

Another way we damage forests is by air **pollution**. Factories and power stations give off dirty fumes. They mix with tiny drops of water in the air, and form acid rain. On wet or foggy days, the acid rain lands on trees. It kills their leaves and weakens them so they are less able to fight disease.

Disappearing forests

The world's forests are shrinking fast. In the last 300 years, the area of land that is covered by forests has been cut in half.

Forests are important

Forests are important for Earth's **climate**. Our planet is getting hotter as a result of **global warming**. This is caused by air **pollution**, which causes a build-up of **carbon dioxide** in the air. Forests can help with this problem. As trees make food for themselves, they remove carbon dioxide from the air. This helps slow down global warming.

These huge logs will be turned into timber.

Tigers in danger

Forests are important for the survival of animals. Amur tigers live in Russia's **coniferous** forests. People have built roads in the forests so they can cut down trees. However, the roads also help others to enter the forest and hunt these rare tigers for their skins.

Good for the environment

Trees are important for the **environment**. Their roots take in rainwater and hold the soil together. When forests are cut down, heavy rain runs away and often causes floods. It also washes the soil away.

Saving the forests

Many people are working to protect forests. Some forests are turned into national parks. Scientists study animals there so they can understand their needs. For example, they put radio collars on **endangered** animals. This helps them to track the animals and protect them from hunters.

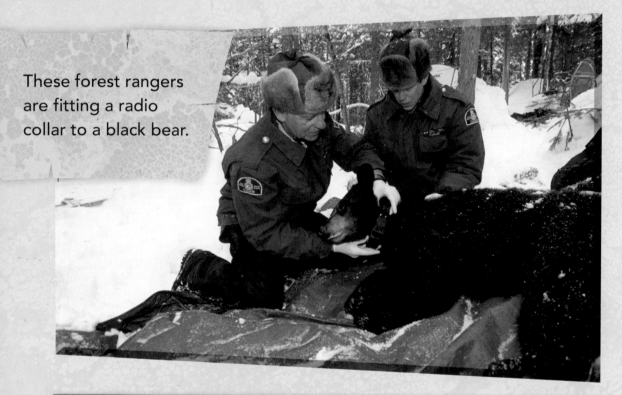

These forest rangers are fitting a radio collar to a black bear.

Planting trees

In the 1970s, Wangari Maathai from Kenya started an organization called the Green Belt Movement. It has helped people in Africa to plant over 40 million trees.

Protecting habitats

People will always need wood. If forests are cared for properly, we can use them responsibly for our own needs as well as protect plant and animal life. In some forests, people plant new trees to replace the trees that have been cut down. These are called sustainable forests.

Tourists pay money to see forest animals. If tourist numbers are controlled, they do not harm these **habitats** and their money can be used to care for the forests. Forests are too important to lose and we must do all we can to protect them.

Glossary

adapt change in order to survive in a particular place

canopy top branches of trees in a forest that are very close together

carbon dioxide gas that is found in air

climate weather pattern in a particular part of the world

conifer evergreen tree that has needle-like leaves and grows its seeds inside cones

coniferous type of forest that contains only conifers

deciduous type of tree that loses its leaves in winter

decomposer animal that eats dead and rotting plants and animals

endangered threatened with dying out

energy power needed to grow, move, and live

environment surroundings in which an animal or plant lives

equator imaginary line around the widest part of Earth, where the weather is always warm

evergreen having leaves all year round

global warming increase in Earth's temperature, caused by chemicals in the air that trap the Sun's heat

habitat place where a plant or animal lives

lichen simple kind of plant that is half-fungus and grows over walls and trees

mammal warm-blooded animal that usually has fur or hair and drinks milk from its mother when it is young

nutrient chemical in food that helps things to grow

poison substance that can cause illness or death

pollution spoiling the air, land, or water with harmful things such as plastic rubbish

prey animal that is hunted and eaten by another animal

temperate area where temperatures are usually mild

thaw become soft as a result of warming up

tropics parts of the world that lie close to the equator

understorey middle layer of a forest, between the canopy and the ground

Find out more

Books
Northern Forests (Habitats), Robert Snedden (Franklin Watts, 2007)

Rainforests (Insiders), Richard C. Vogt (Templar, 2008)

Temperate Forest Habitats (Essential Habitats), Barbara Taylor
 (TickTock, 2009)

Websites
kids.mongabay.com
Find out more about forests, animals, and forest peoples on
this website.

schools.rainforestsos.org
Click on the "Rainforest Sounds" link on this website to listen to
monkeys calling, birds squawking, and insects chirping.

Places to visit

The Eden Project, Bodelva, Cornwall
www.edenproject.com
The Eden Project has a huge greenhouse containing the world's
largest rainforest in captivity with steamy jungles and waterfalls,
colourful tropical plants, and a forest hut.

The Living Rainforest, Hampstead Norreys, Berkshire
www.livingrainforest.org
This rainforest nature park has free-roaming lizards, birds, and
butterflies as well as monkeys, a crocodile, snakes, and much more.

The Royal Botanic Gardens at Kew, London
www.kew.org
Kew Gardens holds over one in eight of all known plants. The
Treetop Walkway takes you through deciduous trees such as
limes and oaks.

Index